ERNEST BERKE

THE NORTH AMERICAN INDIANS

Written and Illustrated by

ERNEST BERKE

Introduction by Frederick J. Dockstader, Director

Museum of the American Indian, New York

THE NORTH AMERICAN
INDIANS

The Indian tribes of North America were different from one another in customs, languages, and religions, but all tribes were alike in their love of the land and their enjoyment of life in harmony with nature. It is true the Indians fought very successfully among themselves, yet when the real battle came to hold the land they owned and loved, they could not band together completely to resist the invasion.

Today, we are indebted to the Indians for numerous foods, agricultural practices, medicines, and games that they developed during their years of freedom in America before the white man came.

DOUBLEDAY & COMPANY, INC.   GARDEN CITY, NEW YORK

INTRODUCTION

The illustrations contained in this volume are the work of a young man who has so thoroughly absorbed the emotion and sensitivity of the West that it comes as something of a surprise to realize his background is almost wholly restricted to the East.

Nevertheless for most of his life Ernest Berke has been painting subjects based on his own careful research and has achieved a place in the Western art world whereby he is totally able to speak on common ground to those who live in the West. I have had the pleasure of working with Mr. Berke from time to time during his preparation of these and many other Western paintings, and I have been impressed by the conscientiousness with which he approaches his paintings. Always careful to be as accurate as possible in ethnographic detail, he at the same time presents his subjects in an artistic manner. I feel that the work in this book can stand close examination by anyone interested in the West—be he student or general reader.

I would unhesitatingly recommend his work to all readers with an interest in the Indian.

FREDERICK J. DOCKSTADER, *Director*
Museum of the American Indian, Heye Foundation
New York, New York

AN IROQUOIS WAR PARTY Dawn on Lake George and a war party, stripped and painted, glides toward the shore to raid an enemy Indian village or a white man's settlement. Crafty Iroquois such as these terrorized the entire Northeast during the years of the French and Indian War (1754–63).

WHEN WAR CRIES RANG   The backwoodsmen of the Alleghenies were the first white men to settle the frontier land of Pennsylvania and Kentucky. All around them lurked hostile Indians, hawk-eyed and wolf-hearted.

INDIANS OF THE NORTHEAST

Principal Tribes

ABNAKI	MOHICAN	OTTAWA
ALGONKIN	MENOMINEE	PENOBSCOT
CAYUGA	MIAMI	PEQUOT
DELAWARE	MICMAC	POTAWATOMI
EASTERN CREE	MOHAWK	SAUK-FOX
ERIE	NARRAGANSET	SENECA
HURON	NIPISSING	SUSQUEHANNA
IROQUOIS	OJIBWA	TUSCARORA
ILLINOIS	ONEIDA	WINNEBAGO
KICKAPOO	ONONDAGA	WYANDOT

I N the Northeast lived the powerful Iroquois Indians. They were enemies to many neighboring tribes and they waged fierce wars with bows and arrows and *tomahawks*. The goal of war was to prove courage and power. And the hope of every Indian boy was to prove himself courageous in battle, in the hunt, and in sport.

When the warriors were not out on raiding parties, they lived with their families in small villages. In the Northeast, the Indians built "longhouses" of logs, saplings, and elm bark. These houses were sixty feet long and eighteen feet wide. Each one could hold six or eight Indian families.

Near the villages, the Northeast Indians grew squash, pumpkins, and beans in small planted fields. But their main food was corn, which in Iroquois language was called "our life."

In the Northeast, women did the farming. They planted and harvested the crops while the men hunted in the woods for moose, bear, deer, and rabbit.

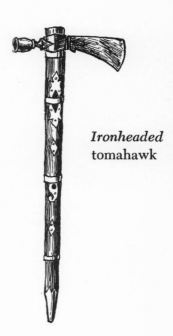

Ironheaded tomahawk

Hoeing corn

E. BERKE

Moccasin

Spoon

The Iroquois wore simple clothing, which the women made by sewing animal skins together. In the summer the men wore breech-cloths, or aprons, of tanned deerskin. They did not need more clothes except for ceremonies or for war when they put on deerskin leggings. For shoes most Indians used moccasins. The women wore skirts of buckskin with fringes on them and short capes, which they draped over their shoulders. On their clothes the Iroquois women did beautiful embroidery with colored porcupine quills and tiny beads traded by the French settlers.

In the winter the Indians wore fur robes made from bear and moose skins. When the white settlers came from England and France they traded wool blankets for Indian furs, which they wanted to sell in Europe.

The settlers were glad to come to America. The land was big enough for many men. There were lakes and wild rivers full of fish. The hunting was good. Settlers from Holland traded rifles to the Indians in the Northeast. Most tribes learned to use rifles for fighting wars.

Indian ways were strange to the white men. Indians lived by the laws of nature. They believed that all good luck and bad luck came from the gods that lived in nature—in a tree or a cloud or a fire. Indians prayed to their gods to watch over the fields of corn and give them meat to eat. Often they danced for the gods in great ceremonies. When the settlers arrived they were surprised at the Indians' religion and tried to teach them about the white man's God. But the Indians did not change their beliefs for many years; they loved the religion that was natural to them.

Iroquois "longhouse"

The Northeast Indians held council meetings to discuss raids and treaties and trades. Five tribes banded together to form the League of the Iroquois. These tribes devised the first democratic government known in North America. Each man had an equal voice in all decisions.

For speaking in council the Iroquois used *wampum* belts woven of hand-cut shell beads. Wampum belts were the records of history. In symbolic designs they preserved the whole of Iroquois wisdom and experience.

Wampum *belt*

Lacrosse

"Snow snake"

All Indians played games. Lacrosse was an Iroquois game that is still played in America today. Throwing the "snow snake" was another Iroquois pastime. The "snake" was a smoothed, waxed rod five to nine feet long that was thrown down an iced groove in the snow—sometimes for a distance of five hundred yards. The longest throw won the game.

Gambling was also fun for the Indians. In the East, a dice game was played with different-colored sticks or bones. On the Plains, another gambling game was played with one stone and three moccasins. Each gambler in his turn had to guess which moccasin hid the stone. In the excitement of the game, Indians often gambled away all their possessions and even their wives.

THE END OF THE PORTAGE A French fur trapper and his Ojibwa guides and porters carry their canoes, furs, and other gear from one body of water to another. They hope to find a water course that will take them down to Quebec or Montreal to sell their fine beaver skins.

On the Canadian shores of the northern Great Lakes lived the Ojibwa Indians. They were hunters and trappers who enjoyed the stillness of the woods. Like the animals they hunted, the Ojibwa could see far into a thicket and hear even a twig snap.

The Ojibwa trapped bear, beaver, marten, and mink for furs to make warm clothes. When the white men arrived, the Ojibwa traded furs for European rifles to defend their lands against the Iroquois.

Otter fur hat

Ojibwa wigwam

Snowshoe

For food the Ojibwa had plenty of ducks and geese as well as bear, moose, and deer. They harvested wild rice that grew at the shores of shallow woodland lakes. Also they grew corn and farm crops like the Iroquois. In the winter, when food was scarce, Indians of enemy tribes sometimes hunted side by side to keep their families alive.

The name Ojibwa, which the French and English settlers called Chippewa, may have come from an Indian word meaning "pictograph maker," or someone who writes with an alphabet of pictures. The Ojibwa learned how to write down ancient legends by drawing pictures on long scrolls of birch bark cut from nearby trees. They used these scrolls like storybooks, and when the young men of the tribe were old enough to join the Ojibwa religious society they listened to the same legends their fathers had learned before them.

The Ojibwa believed that gods spoke to them in dreams. When a member of the tribe became sick, the priests, or *shamans*, put on ugly masks to scare the wicked spirits of sickness away. For all Indians any sickness was a hardship. Each man and woman was needed to work for the family.

Shamans' *masks*

14

Ojibwa hunter

Some Ojibwa families lived in birch bark *wigwams,* or small round houses that came to a point on top. The birch bark was tied onto wooden poles with pieces of spruce root fiber that had been boiled in fish broth until it was soft.

Ojibwa canoes were also made of birch bark that was sewn together and sealed with spruce tree gum and charcoal. The birch bark was laid in a shallow pit and the wood frame of the canoe was fitted inside it, piece by piece. During the fur-trading era, the Ojibwa built canoes thirty-six feet long that could carry twelve men and three tons of cargo.

OSCEOLA'S DEFIANCE In 1834 the United States tried to force the Seminoles to move to the Oklahoma Indian reservation. Osceola, one of their greatest chiefs, sliced the treaty to ribbons, starting a bloody seven-year war that cost the United States Government millions of dollars and the lives of hundreds of soldiers.

INDIANS OF THE SOUTHEAST

Principal Tribes

APALACHEE	CHICKASAW	PAMUNKEY
BILOXI	CHOCTAW	POWHATAN
CADDO	CREEK	SEMINOLE
CATAWBA	MUSKHOGEAN	SHAWNEE
CHEROKEE	NATCHEZ	TUSCARORA

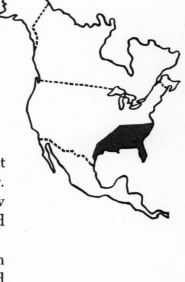

No one knows all the long history of the Southeast Indians. At one time they tattooed their bodies and stuck feathers in their hair. But when the white settlers arrived, the Indians had adopted new fashions—short skirts and leggings for the men and long skirts and blouses for the women.

The Indians of the Southeast were farmers. They lived in a warm climate that was good for growing fruits and vegetables. They did not move their villages from place to place. Nor did they set out on long war parties as the Iroquois and the Ojibwa did. In the Southeast, wars were local affairs, fought between near neighbors.

The farms of the Southeast grew as large as plantations, covering many acres. The strongest chiefs in some tribes kept Indian slaves to do the hard work of hoeing and harvesting the fields. They grew many kinds of beans, squash, and corn. Strawberries and grapes grew wild for picking.

The white settlers in America counted fifteen different kinds of corn grown by the Indians in the North and Southeast. Ears of corn were roasted in the village fires. Corn kernels were dried and ground into corn meal in a mortar and pestle made of heavy wood. Corn meal was used for making bread and a rich, yellow mush. Often the Indians carried a small pouch of dried corn kernels for food when they were away from their villages.

The Southeast Indians sometimes built their houses of wood logs. Where the ground was soft and marshy, they put their houses on wooden stilts to keep the floor dry and keep the snakes away. In the Southeast there were many animals, like snakes and alligators, that loved the warm sunshine and the dark green jungle shadows. There was plenty of wild game on the loose, which the Indian men hunted with bows and arrows.

Mortar and pestle

In the year 1541, when the Spanish explorer de Soto landed in America, he found that the Indians of the Southeast prayed to the sun as their god. They built temples for sun worshiping on huge mounds that marked the graves of their forefathers. They made human sacrifices to please the sun, their "brother," who gave warmth and good harvests and flowers to the land.

But a hundred years after de Soto's visit, sun worshiping had died out. A time of change had begun for the Indians. More and more white men were sailing to America from France, England, and Spain. The Indians looked to the settlers for new knowledge. However, Sequoyah, a chief of the Cherokee tribe, taught himself reading and writing without the help of European settlers. Independently he invented an alphabet for the language used by his people—a feat seldom attempted and accomplished in the history of mankind. Sequoyah hoped that the Cherokee and the white men could live side by side in America and learn from one another. But the settlers were impatient to claim the American land for their own. Fierce wars broke out and many Indians were killed defending their hunting grounds and villages.

Sun worshiping temple

Sequoyah

Tecumseh

Tecumseh of the Shawnee tried in vain to unite the Southeast tribes against the settlers. But the peace-loving tribes would not fight at all and the warrior tribes could not be organized in time to resist the strong white enemy. Osceola, one of the bravest chiefs of any tribe, led his Seminoles through years of battle. In the end, most of the Seminoles were driven to government reservations in the new state of Oklahoma. A few Seminoles, still led by Osceola, continued to fight in the Florida Everglades, where their descendants live to-day.

THE BLACKFOOT STORYTELLER   Indian children listen in wonder as an aged warrior retells the glory of his youth and the legends of his ancient people.

INDIANS OF THE PLAINS

Principal Tribes

ARAPAHO	CROW	OSAGE
ARIKARA	DAKOTA (SIOUX)	OTO
ASSINIBOIN	GROS VENTRE	PAIUTE
BLACKFOOT	HIDATSA	PAWNEE
CADDO	IOWA	PONCA
CAYUSE	KIOWA	SARCEE
CHEYENNE	MANDAN	SHOSHONI
COMANCHE	MISSOURI	UTE
CREE	OMAHA	WICHITA

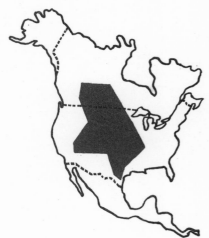

THE Indians of the Plains were buffalo hunters and horsemen. They lived active lives following the herds, stealing horses from each other, dancing, and making war.

Until the Spaniard Coronado came to America in 1540 no Plains Indians had ever seen a horse. At that time, many tribes were moving westward. Their travel was slow because they used dogs to carry their belongings on *travois*. The Indians made their travois by tying two poles onto the dogs' shoulders. Then they rigged wooden slats between the poles and loaded their possessions on top. When the dogs trotted forward, they dragged the poles on the ground behind

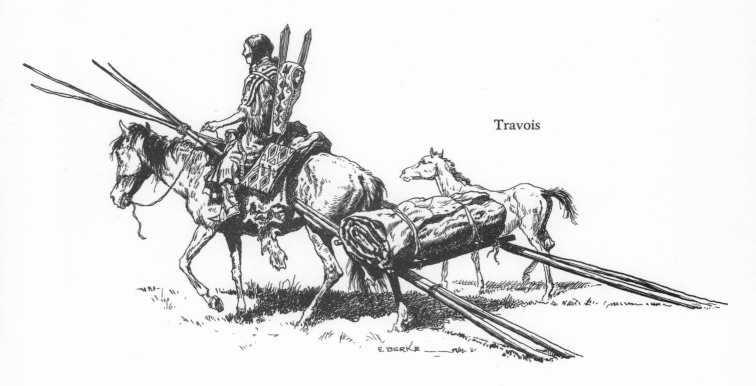

Travois

E. BERKE

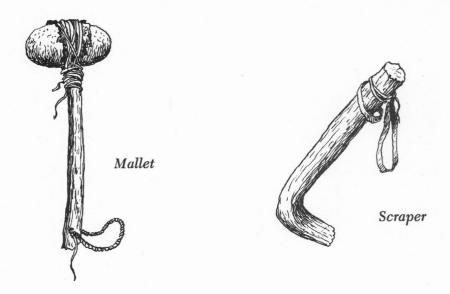

Mallet

Scraper

them. With horses, however, the long journeys across the Plains became easier. The Southern tribes were the first to learn riding from the Spaniards, but by 1750 horses were common all over the Plains.

The Indians learned to hunt on horseback. They learned to circle small buffalo herds and down the outside animals with spears or bows and arrows. The Indians seldom killed more buffaloes than they needed for food. Only after the white men came did the Indians kill foolishly to trade buffalo hides for rifles.

On the Plains, Indian women did the job of butchering the buffaloes. They skinned the animals with sharp knives while wolves and coyotes whined hungrily at a distance. Buffalo meat, fat, and marrow were eaten. Meat that could not be used immediately was cut into thin strips and hung in the sun to dry. The dried meat was then pounded into a pulp with a mallet, mixed with crushed berries—

Skinning buffalo

THE HORSE THIEF Stealing horses was one way to gain great wealth on the Plains. Success enabled a warrior to marry and have influence among his people.

pits and all—and covered with a layer of fat to keep it fresh. This mixture was called *pemmican*. It was kept in rawhide *parfleche* cases to be eaten in the winter when food was scarce.

The Indians used buffalo skulls in ceremonies as symbols of good hunts. From buffalo hoofs and horns they made decorations or rattles. Bones were made into arrowheads, gambling dice, and scrapers for cleaning hides. From buffalo sinews the Indians made thread for sewing and strings for their hunting bows.

Drying buffalo meat

THE BLACKFOOT TRACKER   A Blackfoot hunter in winter clothing
moves along rapidly, intently watching the trail of another horseman or perhaps a moose or buffalo bull.

THE BUFFALO HUNT The Plains Indians trained their fastest and most agile horses for buffalo hunting. A buffalo often tried to hook the horse or rider with his horns while stampeding at breakneck speed. In the midst of a frightened herd, this Plains hunter tries to outrun a bull that has gotten between him and an already wounded cow.

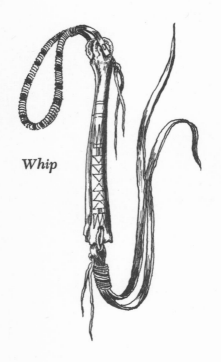

Whip

Buffalo hides had many uses. Untanned rawhide was used for saddles, braided ropes, and parfleche cases. To make heavy winter clothing, the hair was removed from the hides by using scrapers. Then the hides were rubbed and rubbed to soften them. For blankets, the Indians used tanned buffalo skins with the hair left on.

Tepee covers were made of twelve to fourteen tanned buffalo hides sewn together. Tepees were the houses used by many Plains tribes. They were made and owned by the women in each Indian family. Tepees were easy to take down and set up in traveling camps. A tepee had no floor except the earth; but with a fire in the center, the house stayed warm on the coldest winter night. Smoke flaps at the peak of the tepee could be turned away from the wind so the draft would keep the fire burning nicely. In the summertime, the bottom edges of the tepee were rolled up about a foot to let cool breezes inside.

THE EVENING WAR PRAYER   A chief asks the aid of the gods before an undertaking. The evening before his war party departs, he prays and asks "his medicine" to protect him, his pony, and his tribesmen in the adventure to come.

THE PINK PARASOL   A victory celebration on horseback sweeps wildly back and forth before a Plains village. The chiefs parade the scalps and a lady's parasol taken during the massacre of a wagon train or settlement.

Saddle

Plains pipe and bag

NECK AND NECK Horse racing was one of the favorite sports of the
Plains Indians. Riding bareback and whipping fiercely, two young Mandans
fight it out for first place. The spectators stand around and on top of their
large earth lodges.

Wichita grasshouse

On the Plains some tribes did not live in tepees. The Wichita Indians built houses of sticks and grass that looked like giant beehives. These houses were planned for one family. The Mandans built larger houses, or lodges, of earth that was packed onto sturdy wooden frames. They were big enough for the horses and dogs to sleep inside with the family. From a distance, Mandan lodges looked like low hills on the prairies.

While the men were away hunting or fighting wars, the women tanned the hides of deer, elk, and antelope as well as buffalo. They collected wood for their fires, they nursed their children, and even found time for embroidering clothes for the men to wear in the great dances.

Indian babies were carried in *papoose* cradles strapped to their mothers' backs. When they were old enough, boys and girls helped with work around the Indian camp. They did not have a school to go to, so they learned by watching and listening to their parents and grandparents. Indian families were happy living together.

Papoose *cradle*

THE EVENING SERENADE After the day's activity of ceremonies and dances, young men and boys, sometimes three or four on a pony, circle the camp singing a special evening song. This is a Crow Indian village; however, most of the Plains tribes had a similar custom.

Shield

CHEYENNE MARRIAGE After wooing his young girl, a warrior gives a number of horses, beads, blankets, or even a prized rifle to the father of the bride. Wrapped in a sacred painted wedding robe, the warrior proudly leads the bride to his *tepee*.

The camp life of the Plains tribes was highly organized. Both men and women belonged to societies or clubs that were divided by age group. There were societies of warriors called "Dog Soldiers" who acted as a police force, helping to settle arguments within the tribes. Governing chiefs also had societies. In many tribes, chiefs were elected by their people. They were not always the bravest warriors or the swiftest runners. Chiefs were chosen for their wisdom.

DOG SOLDIER DANCE The "Dog Soldiers" were members of a brave
warrior society. When a group decision was made to stand fast in a battle,
each member would plant his spear through a hole at the end of his sash.
Pinned to the spot, he would fight until dead or rescued by a comrade.

War bonnet

A MODEL OF SAVAGE SPLENDOR A handsome warrior returns home
with the prizes of battle: a fine rifle and a U.S. soldier's horse.

MOURNING HER WARRIOR A young woman buries her dead husband after the fashion of the Plains Indians. The warrior is dressed in his finest clothes and wrapped in skins and blankets to ward off hungry birds and animals. The warrior has his weapons, his *pemmican* in a *parfleche* case, and his sacred buffalo skull. The woman will kill his favorite horse under the scaffold, and he will then have all he needs for the journey to the "after-life." She cuts off her long hair, or even a finger, in memory of his death.

Spear

Gunstock tomahawk

ONE DOWN Cheyenne warriors retreat in confusion at seeing one of their number knocked down. The white men, armed with powerful rifles, make their stand a couple of hundred yards away.

Warriors of the Plains went on many raids. The practice of raiding was the warriors' way of earning fame. Each man hoped to touch his enemy with a *coupstick* or with his bare hand before he killed him. Killing enemies was not so important as proving bravery at arm's length.

Plains warriors collected the scalps of their enemies. Scalps were paraded on long spears while the warriors acted out the events of each raid in a wonderful ceremony. All warriors were proud of their bravery; they boasted about it, and their wives and children listened to battle tales with eagerness. On the Plains, war was a game with very serious rules. The highest goal of fighting was to win glory for the individual and the tribe.

The white settlers did not understand the rules of Indian war-making. To them the Indians were dangerous savages. To the Indians the settlers were thieves who came to rob them of their homes and lands. In protest the Indians made war on all white men—settlers and soldiers—who invaded the Plains.

Smoking a pipe

BAD MEDICINE Sometimes the warriors' "good medicine" would forsake them, and they would return from a raid with nothing to show for it but the dead and wounded.

THE SMOKE SCREEN From time to time treacherous raids by U.S. soldiers resulted in the massacre of many Indian women, children, and old people. Whenever possible they were removed from the battle areas under cover of grass smoke. Fire was a great ally of the Indian and he was expert in its use.

Pouch for flint

The Indians knew how to "hit and run," charging out of the hills on fast ponies to take the white men by surprise. Indians could also send messages and warnings to one another over many miles. They used puffs of smoke as a code, which white men seldom understood. For signaling, the Indians needed only a blanket and a fire. No warrior would tell the meaning of a code, even under torture or threat of death.

The most famous battle between the Plains Indians and the U. S. Army took place in 1876 at the Little Bighorn River in Montana. Lieutenant Colonel George Custer led his troops into a Sioux Indian camp on the riverbank. Custer planned to move the Indians off their land, but the Sioux resisted. Many soldiers, including Custer, were killed in the fight. All over the Plains similar battles were fought and men and women died needlessly.

Smoke signals

THE EMIGRANT TRAIL   White settlers traveling west abandoned many belongings for which the Indians had no use. Even today there are places on the prairie where the grass will not grow in the wagon ruts.

During the years of war between the Indians and the white men the great buffalo herds began to disappear. In 1867, the Union Pacific Railroad hired a professional hunter to kill meat for its workers. The hunter's name was "Buffalo Bill" Cody. He killed 4280 buffaloes in eighteen months. The railroad ran special trains so that passengers could shoot into the herds from the car windows; buffalo killing became a sport. By 1884, only two dozen out of sixty million buffaloes were left alive on the Plains.

Many tribes of Plains Indians grew sick from white man's diseases. They grew hungry because the buffaloes were dying. They grew tired of fighting for their lives. Soon the Indians lost the strength and happiness that had been theirs in America before the white man came.

Buffalo skull

THE SEARCH
White men killed millions of buffaloes for the hides and tongues, and the Indians went hungry. By 1884 the bones of buffaloes and other animals whitened the prairies like snow. In North Dakota, one bone pile alone was said to weigh five thousand tons.

42

THE SANDSTORM For many years the livelihood of the Navahos was dependent almost entirely upon sheep. The loss of a single animal was a serious matter, especially to the young herder who was responsible for their safety.

INDIANS OF THE SOUTHWEST

Principal Tribes

ACOMA	MOHAVE	TONTO
APACHE	NAVAHO	WALAPAI
HAVASUPAI	PAPAGO	YAQUI
HOPI	PIMA	YUMA
JAMEZ	PUEBLO	ZUÑI
LAGUNA	TAOS	
MARICOPA	TARAHUMARE	

ANCESTORS of the Southwest Indians built the first cliff dwellings, or pueblos, in America. The pueblos were made of stone and "adobe" —a clay that hardens like cement when dried in the sun. Today's Pueblo Indians still live in the traditional houses of old, which are big enough for a whole village of families.

Pueblo land was a treeless desert. The weather was hot in summer and cold and windy in winter. Very little rain fell throughout the year, so the Pueblo Indians dug ditches to catch all the water they could for their crops. In the Southwest the men did the farming. The work was hard. Yet the Pueblos grew six colors of corn, as well as cotton, beans, and squash.

Pueblo

Making pottery

Pueblo women worked on weaving blankets and baskets. They also made fine clay pots, which they formed from a long roll of clay coiled like a snake. With their hands the women smoothed the ridges of the coil and coated each pot with a thin layer of another clay called "slip." This coating was then painted with many bright colors and the pot was baked in adobe brick ovens until it was hard.

The religion of the Southwest honored the gods of rain, good harvests, and good health. The Pueblo Indians belonged to the *Kachina* Cult, which had a special way of worshiping. The Pueblos believed the Kachinas were half god and half man. They prayed to the Kachinas to speak for them to the highest gods. Pueblo prayers took the form of great dancing ceremonies led by the shamans, or medicine men of the tribe. These dances were taken very seriously. They were not for fun. The dancers dressed in brilliant costumes and strange masks to look like the Kachinas themselves were thought to look. The dancers believed the Kachinas were with them in spirit as they performed.

Grinding corn

THE KACHINA CARVER A Hopi Indian craftsman makes brightly painted wooden dolls that look like the *Kachina* dancers dressed for the great rain ceremonies.

For many years the Pueblo Indians lived in peace. They loved to care for their crops, work on their handicrafts, and practice their religion. Wars were few and far between because most Southwest tribes were too busy farming to have time for fighting.

THE SNAKE DANCE   This dance is held each year to invoke the gods to make rain. The dancers are seldom bitten by the diamondback rattlers because another dancer, called a *hugger*, distracts the snake's attention with a feather wand. The snake, after being released, is supposed to tell the gods of the Hopi's desperate need for rain.

The Navaho Indians did like to make war, however. Navaho warriors raided many tribes in the Southwest, including the quiet Pueblos. The Navahos moved about with their flocks of sheep and never settled in villages. For this reason they learned many customs from other Southwest tribes and became skilled in many crafts.

Navaho women were fine weavers. They made beautiful wool blankets on wooden looms that stood upright in the sand. The wool threads were dyed many bright colors by using vegetable dyes. From the early Spanish explorers the Navahos learned how to hammer silver into jewelry. The men made necklaces, bracelets, and belts of silver inlaid with small turquoise stones chipped from the rocks of the desert.

Sand painting

From the Pueblo Indians the Navahos learned the sand-painting ceremony. This was a magic rite to cure disease. The sand painting, sometimes as big as fifteen feet across, was made of different colors of sand sprinkled in a design on the floor of a hut called a *hogan*. After one use, the painting was destroyed. The magic power of the design lasted only a day.

The Apache Indians were wanderers like the Navahos. They did not care about farming and growing crops, though some Apache women kept small gardens and grew corn. They lived in the hills where they shot deer and mountain lions for their food. They often went on long hunts into buffalo country where they would kill as many animals as they could and then carry the meat back to the hills on their horses.

Weaving a blanket

The Apaches used tepees or *wickiups* for their houses. A wickiup was a low shelter made of saplings and covered with grass mats or animal skins. It was big enough for one family. Whenever the Apaches moved camp they left most of their houses behind.

Apache Indians loved war. They fought against the Spaniards, the first white men to travel in the Southwest. They fought against other tribes around them. And they fought against the American settlers and the U. S. Army. Apache warriors trained for battle like athletes. Boys were made to run several miles in the heat with a mouthful of water that was not to be swallowed. At the end of the run, the boys had to spit out every drop of the water. Young warriors also learned how to be quick and agile by dodging arrows fired at them by their trainers.

The Apaches had good eyesight. They could see a long way from secret crannies in the rocks. No Indians in North America were as skilled as the Apaches at hunting and tracking their enemies over the harsh country of the desert.

One famous Apache, the warrior Geronimo, played a hide-and-seek game with the U. S. Army for fourteen years. Like many Indians in North America, Geronimo would not give up his freedom without a fight.

Apache "Devil Dance"

THE CROOKED TRAIL It was difficult to trail someone in wild Apache territory. If the trail was obscure to these sharp-eyed trackers, it must have been made by another Apache who was even more clever in covering up his tracks.

SPRING At a point where Idaho, Oregon, and Washington meet, the mountain slopes are covered with wild flowers from early spring to late fall. An old woman of the Nez Perce tribe gathers firewood while the crows flapping over the hill scold her for disturbing them.

INDIANS OF THE COLUMBIA PLATEAU

Principal Tribes

COEUR D'ALENE	NEZ PERCE	UMATILLA
FLATHEAD	PALOUSE	WALLA WALLA
KALISPEL	SPOKAN	YAKIMA
KUTENAI	TENINO	

IN 1805, the famous Lewis and Clark Expedition arrived at the Columbia River in Idaho. It was met by the Nez Perce Indians. A friendly tribe, the Nez Perces were hunters and river fishermen. Their name meant "pierced noses." It was given to them by the French fur trappers who thought the Indians wore pieces of shell in their noses for decoration.

The Plateau Indians liked to eat buffalo meat. Often they journeyed to the Plains and traded horses for buffalo meat and hides. The Nez Perce and the Palouse tribes were good horsemen. The Palouse bred a special kind of pony—the Appaloosa—which was small and sure-footed. They used their ponies for hunting and trading. Some tribes traveled as far west as the Pacific Coast on trading trips.

Besides buffalo meat, the Plateau Indians ate elk, white mountain goat, and bear, as well as Columbia River salmon, roots, and the bulb of the camass lily.

The clothing of the Plateau tribes was similar to the Plains Indians'. When the winter was cold they wrapped themselves in thick blankets. They wore clothes made of tanned animal hides. The Plateau women often wore straw hats like baskets to protect themselves from the summer sun.

When a tribe was traveling, families slept in tepees. Otherwise the Plateau Indians built lodges covered with woven grass mats or small huts made of sod. Villages were often built near the Columbia River to be close to the salmon fishing grounds.

The tribes of the Plateau were all friendly to the first white settlers.

Many Indians helped them over the high mountain passes as Sacagawea had done for Lewis and Clark. Sacagawea was a girl of the Shoshoni tribe. She was strong and courageous and she traveled west with the expedition to act as a guide. On the journey Sacagawea gave birth to a baby whom Lewis and Clark befriended.

Camass bulbs

THE VISION SEEKER Each young man in an Indian tribe went out alone to seek the spirit that would guard over him through his life. The seeker went without food for four days. Finally his vision would come—a bird or animal or strange spirit from Indian legend—to flood him with its power.

OH, GRAY WOLF OF MY TRIBE, I TOO AM HUNTING Indians often asked aid of the animals around them. A lone hunter in the snowy mountains of the Plateau asks the wolves, the greatest of all animal hunters, to help him find food.

Chief Joseph

The Plateau Indians wanted to know of the white man's religion. They wanted to learn reading and writing. But after a while the white settlers were crowding out the Indians and taking over the Indian lands. Many Plateau tribes turned from their friendly ways to hold the settlers back.

The hero of the Plateau Indians was a man named Chief Joseph. He led the Nez Perces across a thousand miles of wild country hoping to find safety in Canada. But the brave Nez Perces were surrounded by U.S. soldiers only thirty miles from the Canadian border.

Chief Joseph's speech of surrender told of the sadness in his heart. "I am tired of fighting. Our chiefs are dead. The old men are all dead. He who led the young men is dead. It is cold and we have no blankets. The little children are freezing to death. My people, some of them, have run away to the hills and have no blankets, no food, no one knows where they are. I want to have time to look for my children and see how many I can find. Hear me, my chiefs. From where the sun now stands I will fight no more forever."

SALMON FISHING Salmon, migrating up the Columbia River to spawn and die, were caught by spear, net, or trap by the Plateau Indians. Each fishing spot was guarded by the family that owned it, for salmon was their most important food and trade item.

THE WHALER'S ANCESTORS All the people of the Northwest Coast were good fishermen, but the Nootka were the great whalers. In a secret shrine containing the skulls and *totem* carvings of his relatives, a chief prays for good fortune in the coming expedition.

INDIANS OF THE NORTHWEST COAST

Principal Tribes

BELLA COOLA	KWAKIUTL	SONGISH
CHIMAKUAN	NISQUALLI	SQUAMISH
CHINOOK	NOOTKA	TILLAMOOK
COMOX	PAYALL UP	TLINGIT
DUWAMISH	SALISH	TSIMSHIAN
HAIDA	SHAHAPTIAN	TWANA
KUSA	SNOHOMISH	YONKALLA

Totem *pole*

ALONG the beautiful Northwest Coast lived an amazing group of Indian tribes. They were fishermen, traders, and wood carvers. One tribe, the Tlingit, lived far north close to the Eskimos of Alaska. This tribe was the first to see the Russian fur traders who came to America around 1750. The Northwest Coast was rich with hair seal, otter, marten, fox, bear, and ermine.

The Northwest Indians spent their lives on the sea and in the coastal mountains. Each tribe had its own fishing ground, which was guarded for its chief and his children. The Indians had plenty of fish and seaweed for their food. But they also ate roots and berries and the meat of small woodland animals. The Northwest Indians were good rock climbers. They could creep up on an unsuspecting mountain goat and kill it with a spear.

When the Russian traders arrived they showed the Northwest tribes chisels and cutting tools made of iron. But for many years the Indians had carved *totem* poles using tools of flint and shell. The Indians made their houses of cedar planks. Totem poles stood at the corners or doorways of these houses. Covered with strange faces and animal figures, totem poles told the history and ancestry of each chief in the clan. Sometimes the poles were so large that the doorway to a house was cut right through them.

From the big trees that grew in the Northwest, the Nootka Indians carved their whaling canoes. These canoes were thirty to fifty feet long. They were built for hard use and could carry eight or more men. When a whale was sighted, the hunters paddled their canoes in close to its head to get the best shots with their weapons. The bravest men jumped onto the whale's back for the kill. Nootka hunters used harpoons like the Eskimos. Each harpoon had a long rope attached to it so that the harpooned whale would drag the hunters' canoes along until it tired. Floats made of sealskin were tied onto the harpoon rope to keep the whale from diving deep into the water. After the kill, the whale was towed slowly back to land. Whale meat and fat could feed many families for many weeks.

The Northwest Indians wore blankets woven of shredded cedar bark and the hair of mountain goats or dogs. They traded these blankets from tribe to tribe and took much pride in the weaving of them. When the white traders came, the Indians began trading furs for wool blankets from Europe. These were very valuable to the Indians. Soon they were using wool blankets like money. The more blankets a chief owned, the wealthier he was.

In the Northwest, tribes were very warlike and competitive. They competed for riches according to an interesting custom. The chief of one tribe would invite a rival chief to a great party called a *potlatch*. To get the feast ready the whole tribe would work for many weeks. The host would give gifts to his guest. Sometimes he burned his own valuable blankets and killed his own slaves just to show the guest that possessions meant nothing to him. The host tried to appear very wealthy. After the potlatch, the guest chief was expected to give a greater feast in return. His whole tribe would prepare a new potlatch. But if he did not outdo the first party, his tribe was disgraced.

Totem *pole*

Potlatch

THE BEAR CLAN COMES CALLING   A Kwakiutl canoe bearing messengers comes to announce a *potlatch* or perhaps a wedding. The chief, in bearskins and mask, stands in the prow as the men sing songs of greeting.

A DESPERATE SITUATION California Indian women and children were often terrified by the many bears in the nearby forests. They escape here leaving a lone hunter to battle a six-hundred-pound grizzly.

INDIANS OF CALIFORNIA

Principal Tribes

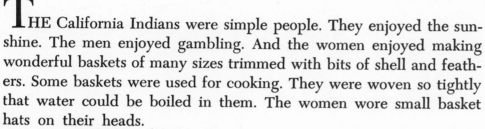

CHUMASH	MAIDU	SHASTA
HUPA	MIWOK	WAPPO
KAROK	MODOC	WASHO
KATO	MONO	YOKUT
KLAMATH	POMO	YUROK

THE California Indians were simple people. They enjoyed the sunshine. The men enjoyed gambling. And the women enjoyed making wonderful baskets of many sizes trimmed with bits of shell and feathers. Some baskets were used for cooking. They were woven so tightly that water could be boiled in them. The women wore small basket hats on their heads.

In the north, the men fished in the ocean and the rivers or hunted in the deep forest shade. For stalking game they bathed themselves in smoke and wore deerskins for disguises. In the south, the Indians kept farms. They ate berries, as well as corn, beans, and squash. Many tribes collected acorns and ground acorn flour for making bread and soup.

Basket weaver

One of the first tribes to see white men was the Chumash, who lived along the Santa Barbara coast. This tribe built villages of dome-shaped houses made of willow poles covered with woven reed mats. The houses had many rooms, and forty or more Indians slept in each one on beds like bunks. The Chumash also built canoes twelve to twenty-five feet long out of driftwood planks. They sewed the planks together with fiber chords and sealed the cracks with asphalt.

The California Indians made no wars. They wanted peace even after the white men came. Many Indians lived happily in the Spanish missions that were built in California after 1769. All Indians wanted to stay on the land of their forefathers. But the white men had already claimed America for themselves. And the Indians had to bow before the white men or be killed. In the end, the conflict between the white man and the Indian arose over land—the richest, yet the most plentiful treasure of the New World.